WISDOM
FOR THE WEEK

John L Keyes

Wisdom for the Week / J. Keyes.
First Edition

ISBN: 978-1-964963-47-1

Table Of Content

PREFACE

What is Wisdom for the Week?

Wisdom for the Week is a collection of shared thoughts intended to help others navigate the many challenges that are sure to arise in life. It is about ideals that should rightfully be used to help us identify and process strategies each of us must develop and use to achieve our goals. Wisdom for the Week offers thoughts that edify and encourage the human spirit to persevere through life's valleys and, afterward, move onward to victories at the top of countless mountains.

Words are the building blocks of the human spirit. Words infused with faith and encouragement are designed to help us find our calling and live out our destinies. I suggest that each reader meditate on all the "wisdom for the week" pieces to stay focused on their short-term, mid-term, and long-term goals.

Be encouraged!

~ J. Keyes ~

WEEK 1

The Power of Self Encouragement

You can't always depend on having a cheerleader in your corner. When your spirits are down, you might be the only person who can lift them. You may very well need to hear your own voice repeatedly telling you that you will succeed. As you move into higher levels of belief in your own calling, the more the naysayers will attempt to surround you. If your destiny is already yours to take possession of, then the only person required to believe in that destiny is you.

First, get all the naysayers out of your inner circle of influence. Second, do not update naysayers on your progress, even if the news is good. Finally, push yourself to be your number one cheerleader and surround yourself with people who will give you honest feedback and generally agree with your destiny as you have described it to them. Following these three directives will help you walk into a future that reflects who you truly are.

In Acts 9:40, Peter raises Tabitha from the dead. The Amplified Bible states, "But Peter put them all out of the room [the crying widows] and knelt down and prayed; then, turning to the body, he said, 'Tabitha, get up!' And she opened her eyes…" The distraction of doubt was removed from the room before Peter uttered his words of faith. The result was that Peter's words of faith tapped into God's power.

In Matthew 13:54-58 KJVS, Jesus goes into His own country where the inhabitants knew Him and his family. Jesus' countrymen knew Him…so well, they thought, that they were unable to believe that He was the long-awaited Messiah, the Anointed One…the Christ. The scripture goes on to say that "He [Jesus] did not many mighty works there because of their unbelief."

Doubters cannot restrain the manifestation of God's power. God's power is not changed or altered by unbelief. Instead, unbelief can delay the manifestation of God's power until it connects with faith. Unbelief is not trusting God. Unbelief can never thwart the Divine Will of God; yet, it can prevent God from using you to bring His will to pass. If you are not in peak faith condition, surrounding yourself with doubters is the last thing you want to do. Surround yourself with people of strong faith who are interested in helping you bring your vision into clear view.

WEEK 2

Time the Finite Resource

It is true that if you have breath, it is never too late to try something new or change something about yourself. Yet, we must all understand the value of our time. We cannot get back lost time; it is the most valuable commodity that we all have.

In order to learn something that is new and of value to your life, you must be committed to making better use of your work and play time.

If you are to perform at peak levels, you will have to make time for those things that will help you perform at the highest possible levels. This is true for both work and play.

You must make time to think about what you want to accomplish and what you need to do to put specific goals and objectives of your calling into action. First, take care of yourself, the people in your life, and the various relationships you have with the men, women, and children who make up your world and daily life. Your personal goal must be to balance priorities while insisting on personal excellence as the standard. The ability to consistently and properly prioritize, as well as wisely use the time you have, is exactly what will help propel you toward success after success.

I am learning the power of asking God to help me properly prioritize the time He has given me. In the book of 2 Kings, chapter 20, the Prophet Isaiah tells King Hezekiah that he is going to die. Hezekiah's response was to pray to God and remind Him that he had walked before Him in truth and with a perfect heart. In response to Hezekiah's prayer, God added 15 more years to his life. Time is a valuable commodity that you should always talk to God about. Plan to use God's wisdom to help you rightly divide your time.

God is in control of time. He is the Master of time, and no one is more equipped to give us the proper understanding about time and its use than God Himself. Here is a suggestion: For one week, write down everything that you do over the course of each of the seven days. At the end of the week, record the amount or percentage of time each activity took in comparison to the total amount of time spent on all activities. For example, studying for a test might have taken 4 hours, which, in comparison to the time spent on other activities, might have taken 10 percent of your time. Review the total list of activities and the time percentages used. Now, pray about how you are using your time and ask for God's guidance. Then, take the list and adjust it based on how God is prompting you to prioritize your various activities. He will let you know what should be truly important. Remember, you can't take care of others if you do not take care of yourself.

All the work Hezekiah did in the additional 15 years God blessed him with would have been impossible without God's healing grace. Let's do our best to walk in divine health throughout life to make the best use of the time God has given us.

WEEK 3

Carrying the Dead

If you are a divorced person, you may now think of a former marriage as dead and gone. If you tried your hand at a business but it failed, you very likely think of your former business as dead... a thing of the past. In many of these situations, it may be true that someone in your life failed to live up to your expectations of help, work, and support. Maybe you failed to live up to your own expectations. Regardless of the source, the result was the death of a vision and a plan that you had for your life.

In each of the above examples, it is obvious that "death experiences" are not necessarily about the physical loss of a person or thing. Instead, what you and I experience is the death of hopes and our aspirations. What has occurred is the loss of imagination and the loss of belief in a vision of what might have been. Of course, mourning occurs naturally after a loss. It is natural and a necessary part of healing, but then, it is a time when you must leave in the past what is no longer living. Picking up dead things and carrying them around with you will only slow your forward momentum. Dead things will weigh you down and make it harder to get to the finish line. What dead things are you carrying? Put those things down now! Refuse to carry them any longer. Leave them exactly where they belong…in the past. You're alive! So, take your alive self to something new and live!

In Luke 9:60 (KJVS), Jesus spoke to a man, telling him to follow Him, but the man responded that he first needed to bury his father. Jesus replied to him, "Let the dead bury their dead: but go thou and preach the kingdom of God." Jesus is speaking here of the spiritually dead but physically alive, burying those who are both physically and spiritually dead. He told the man to go preach the kingdom of God. Basically, Jesus wanted the man to go and tell people how they could be spiritually alive forever! Jesus' message was that spreading the Gospel was more important than burying someone who was already dead. We are to do the things that breathe life into the lives of those around us. Examine your life. What dead things are you carrying around that steal your peace, joy, and keep you from serving God and living out your own destiny?

Paul helps us understand how Jesus' words are to be applied to our individual lives in Philippians 3 verse 13 when he says, "Brethren, I count not myself to have apprehended; but this one thing I do, forgetting those things which are behind, and reaching forth unto those things which are before, I press toward the mark for the prize of the high calling of God in Christ Jesus." Disconnect from anything and everything that is dead but is still having a negative impact on your ability to press towards the high calling you have in your life!

Write down those things and put them in a sealed envelope. Address the envelope to God. Put the envelope away to never be opened again. Verbally say, "I am casting these past things on Jesus because He cares for me." Then, every time one of the dead issues comes up, remind God that you have already sealed the issue in the envelope and cast that particular care on Him.

Jesus has told you to be anxious for nothing but, by prayer and supplication with thanksgiving, to make your requests known unto God. As Jesus said to the woman at the well, "But whosoever drinketh of the water that I shall give him shall never thirst; but that water that I shall give him shall be a well of water springing up into everlasting life." Now is the time to drink the water of God's Word and focus on the present and the future. The past is for you to learn from not to live in.

WEEK 4

Money Is Always the Answer but Never the Root

If I only had more money, I could......

There is always something we can put into that blank. Money is the answer that almost universally functions as a bridge to something or as the gap filler for the many desire's we humans long for. However, money is almost never the root of an issue or the heart of the matter. Beyond the basic needs of food, shelter, clothes, and water, money motivations are driven by the person in possession of it. Money, in and of itself, is a neutral force. Money takes on the character and ambitions of the person who possesses it. At the heart level, what is your relationship with money? Are your motivations mostly about self? Are they mostly about generosity toward others? Are they about empowering self and others? Wealth makes us more of what we already are on the inside. Therefore, when it comes to money, we must first know thyself. If we understand our heart toward money, we will know how to temper ourselves and make wiser decisions about how to use it. Ecclesiastes chapter 7, verse 12 states, "For wisdom is a defense, and money is a defense: but the excellency of knowledge is, that wisdom giveth life to them that have it." Of course, wisdom is the better of the two in the comparison between wisdom and money. Yet, money used with wisdom can certainly be a defensive weapon. Money can be used to purchase the services of an exceptional lawyer to defend you in an important case. Money can be used to purchase the services of bodyguards with exceptional skill and military training to keep you safe. In Ecclesiastes 10:19, money is a resource that can answer all things in the natural realm. Yet, wisdom is the thing that guides us to the knowledge of the questions that need answers. Wisdom helps us to secure the right answers and guides us in applying the right answers to our daily living. Therefore, godly wisdom functions as the guide for the use of our money.

Expand your thinking by making a concerted effort to understand more about savings, the companies you have invested in through your 401K, income property, business ownership, and the relationship between asset ownership and wealth building. If you spend one hour per week learning about things that pertain to money and wealth building, you will have 52 hours of information to use to make more informed decisions about money in the year following. If you know someone who is trustworthy and has a good handle on their finances, ask that person to mentor you or to be a sounding board for your financial decisions. Good stewardship of money can change your family's life and positively impact the generations that come behind you. Proverbs 13:22 (NIV) says, "A good person leaves an inheritance for their children's children, but a sinner's wealth is stored up for the righteous." You are that good person.

WEEK 5

Remember When

When I was a very young boy, there was a song called "Hold On." Even though I didn't understand the song then the way I do today, it spoke to my spirit even in my youth. Every time I listened to the song, it moved me to tears. I would sometimes avoid listening to it because of the emotional response it drew out of me. Even now, the song reminds me of my journey and still has the power to bring tears to my eyes. It reminds me that the little boy of the past is still inside of me — the simple thoughts of a young boy that were so clear, the love that family members can have for one another, coupled with the struggle to survive, the little boy who wondered why his father never came to see him, the kid who was embarrassed to have his mother send him to the store with food stamps instead of cash. Inside of that boy was a dream that is much clearer in manhood. It is the dream to do something better and be something more than what he was experiencing. The desire to live a better life was in his heart even then. Today, that desire is still there. The desire to be everything I was created to be and nothing less.

Every once in a while, I will play "Hold On" to remind myself to keep on dreaming. I play it to remind myself of the faith it takes to realize your dreams. Most of all, I play it to remind myself to keep holding on. So, remember the experiences that have motivated you. Hold on tightly to your dreams and don't let anything or anyone cause you to lose your grip! Live with the expectation that your dreams will come true!

In Luke 22:19, Jesus instructs us in performing the Last Supper, telling us to do these things in remembrance of Him. God wants us to keep our bond with Him strong. Remembering key events is a crystallizer. Paul reminded Timothy that he must stir up God's gift, which he received when Paul laid hands on him [2 Timothy 1:6]. Remembering is not about living in the past; it is about keeping focused on your calling as you move forward. Remembering what God has done for you fortifies your faith and trust in God for what comes next in your life. Remembering helps you to stay rooted and grounded while stretching to reach the vision that God has placed in your heart.

WEEK 6

Trust vs. Forgiveness

People often get these two values confused. They are not the same thing, and we all need to know the difference. Forgiveness is showing grace to a person who has broken your trust. It is remaining in a relationship with that person despite them having committed a significant wrong against you. Trust is something that comes from observing a person's behavior over time. When a person demonstrates consistent trustworthy behavior, he becomes a person you trust. Trust is not automatic with forgiveness.

Let us say a husband cheats on his wife. When the wife discovers the indiscretion, she is heartbroken. The couple separates for a short time, but ultimately, she decides to forgive her husband. Now, the issue of infidelity is not truly over. Trust must be reinstated into the marriage. He can't be out late into the night without giving an account to his wife. He can't be seen dining with a female without arousing suspicion. This husband can't come home with lipstick on his shirt or a hickey on his neck. Trust is something that is earned.

Forgiveness is an unmerited gift.

What I think is often not talked about as it relates to the Parable of the Talents is the path to becoming trustworthy. The Parable is included in verses 14-28 of chapter 25 in the book of Matthew. The Lord had to know His servants well because He gave them control over His possessions based on their ability. For the two servants to whom the Lord gave 5 talents and 2 talents, He blessed them with a 100% increase. We tend to focus on their increase but not on what their Lord said. The Lord said unto them, "Well done, thou good and faithful servant: thou hast been faithful over a few things, I will make thee ruler over many things; enter thou into the joy of thy Lord." The word that leaped off the page is faithful. Merriam-Webster defines faithful as:

1. Steadfast in affection or allegiance; loyal.
2. Firm in adherence to promises or observance of duty.
3. Given with strong assurance: binding.
4. True to the facts, to a standard, or an original.

The Cambridge Dictionary defines "faithful" as an adjective using the words:

1. trusted; loyal.

In the parable, we see that trust, through specific behaviors, must be established before more responsibility is given. A covenant is a pledge, promise, and bond that is established by trust. When a covenant is broken, the trust is broken. Trust is a precious commodity. Your credit score reflects your trustworthiness to pay back borrowed money. We pay people we owe because we want to reflect God's character. Proverbs 3:27 (NIV) states, "Do not withhold good from those to whom it is due, when it is in your power to act." Trustworthiness is how you want to be seen by the world around you. It is the most important characteristic of your personal brand as you establish business or personal relationships.

Trust is the foundation of agreements, unions, and relationships of every kind, but especially marriage. Nothing worthwhile can be built on an unstable foundation.

WEEK 7

Passionate Exhaustion

Passionate energy directed towards an expected successful end is a good thing! It is passionate energy that fuels the entrepreneur's and leader's heartbeat in a creative start-up company. Let that fire burn as much as you can while the energy remains positive for the company. However, leaders should be on the lookout for signs that the tone of their company's energy has turned negative. It is the leader's responsibility to consistently take the temperature of his team. His goal is to keep members of the team energized, healthy, and honest with one another. The key is to always have your team ready to win in the 4th quarter, with the game tied and only two minutes left to play. Champions are ready for the necessary grind that is needed for the big win!

In Chapter 10 of the Book of Joshua, the Amorites attacked the town of Gibeon, and the men of Gibeon requested Joshua's help. The Lord told Joshua that He had delivered the Amorites into his hands and to not fear them. Israel fought the Amorites to victory, and they fled from Israel."

In the Book of Joshua, chapter 10, verses 12 through 15, Joshua, believing in God's promise of victory, spoke to the Sun and Moon, demanding that they stay still, and the Sun and Moon did not move until Israel had avenged its enemies. Now, that is the way to close out a battle!

Like many other things in life, business is often a battle. We are dealing with competitive forces and weapons used against us. We must keep our teams healthy and confident in their leadership. To have the confidence of those who follow, leadership must operate in transparency and wisdom. Weapons may form, but they will not prosper when the environment is healthy!

WEEK 8

You're an Ultimate Fighting Champ!

Success is a fighting word! For success to be real, it requires overcoming a challenge. Success has infused into the very word the will to persevere. Success has degrees or levels, and it keeps evolving. Success will not stop until it reaches the pinnacle of its goal. True success is never self-destructive. In fact, true success is a beacon that provides a guiding light for those who properly seek it and endeavor to follow and consume the nuggets of wisdom along the successful journeys of others. The gleaning of wisdom from others helps us find our own successful path.

Thought:

If you are in a fight and you are not winning, don't stop fighting!

As he faces death, Paul writes to Timothy, his spiritual son, describing his successful ministry this way: 'I have fought a good fight, I have finished my course, I have kept the faith.'

Paul reminds Timothy that he had experienced suffering firsthand at Antioch, Iconium, and Lystra, and how the Lord had delivered him out of all three situations. In 2 Corinthians 11:25-27, Paul speaks specifically about receiving 39 stripes on five occasions, being beaten with rods, stoned, and shipwrecked. Paul was saying there is no victory without the will to persevere and fight on. Champions fight and stay the course until they achieve success. They learn from their mistakes and self-correct along their journey toward victory. Always study your failures to understand what contributed to them. Ask yourself why the failure happened and what you should have done differently. Once you have completed your evaluation, you can use what you have learned to move forward.

WEEK 9

Have You Made a Decision?

Believing you can do something or become something you have only imagined is fueled by your courage to act on what you believe. Do you believe enough to act? Do you believe enough to go beyond your fear? When you do believe enough to act and move beyond your fear, you step into a realm where all things are possible.

Thought:

Every day that we wake up, we must choose what type of person we are going to be: winner or loser, good or evil, love-filled or hate-filled.

Actions begin with choices. Matthew 6:24 (KJV) says, "No man can serve two masters: for either he will hate the one and love the other; or else he will hold to the one and despise the other. Ye cannot serve God and mammon." Paul further describes these "choices" in Romans 7:21-23 (KJV), "I find then a law that when I do good, evil is present with me. For I delight in the law of God after the inward man. But I see another law in my members, warring against the law in my mind and bringing me into captivity to the law of sin, which is in my members.

Your flesh will never be saved. It is your spirit man that will be saved. The spirit man will receive a new body. Therefore, we must be guided by our spirit man that is tuned into God. We must walk after the guidance of the Holy Spirit. That way, we will not give in to what the flesh wants. Once we get our flesh under subjection, making the correct decisions becomes clearer and easier. The only way to accomplish a clear decision-making mind is by spending time with God in His Word and learning how to apply it to your daily life. We must be vulnerable to the Word of God and allow it to penetrate our hearts. Luke 8:11-15 speaks to the condition of our hearts and ends with the good heart hearing the Word, keeping it, and bringing forth fruit with patience. We need a person of strong faith in our lives as an accountability partner. These are people who we give the right to question our actions and motives.

Remember, courage is confidence in God's ability to do what He says and faith that He will keep His promises. As you make decisions about your life, make those decisions without fear present. Fear has no place in your decision-making process. Be confident in God and be confident in your ability to follow His guidance.

WEEK 10

Circumstances Don't Determine the Outcome, Your Faith Does!

Do not get caught up in an environment that opposes your dreams. You must believe in more than what you can see at a given moment. You must believe in the vision you have inside yourself. Your continual, relentless belief will cause you to manifest the vision inside you. Your vision will be seen in this natural realm because your actions and belief are intertwined. The dream inside you can become the reality you live in.

Thought:

It is the ordinary person who, because of his or her faith steps out of the boat and does the extraordinary.

In Matthew 19, Jesus referred to it being easier for a camel to go through the eye of a needle than for a rich man to enter the kingdom of God. His disciples wanted to know who then could be saved. Jesus said, "With men, this is impossible; but with God, all things are possible."

In Mark 9:23, Jesus further expounds on this thought with the statement, "If you can? Everything is possible for one who believes." Faith that is acted on is the core element needed to experience a vision that actually comes to pass. Hebrews 11:1 in the Amplified Bible says faith is "the assurance (the confirmation, the title deed) of the things we hope for, being the proof of things we do not see and the conviction of their reality [faith perceiving as real fact what is not revealed to the senses]." Faith is the title deed that gives you the rights of ownership. If I have a title with a VIN number for a black, 4-door Dodge Charger, you don't need to see the car to know that I own it. The title is proof that I own the car. It doesn't matter whether the Dodge is 1 block away or 1000 miles away. I still own it. That is exactly how your faith works after God has given you something that you cannot see yet.

WEEK 11

Giants

The only requirement for you to become a giant in anything is for you to become a giant in your inner self first. Internal belief and relentless actions create the inner giant before anyone can see him or her. If the inner self becomes a giant, the outside world will eventually line up and come into agreement. This is always the case. The world will recognize the giant you have become.

Thought:

Transparency and your personal testimony are the most powerful ways to change others' minds.

Revelations 12:11 speaks to the saints overcoming the accuser by the blood of the Lamb and by the words of their testimony. A personal testimony of God's active presence in your life is at the core of every believer's faith. Giant living is a progressive work. It happens with patience and the passing of time. Usually, there is a powerful testimony that is connected to any person who is developing GIANT

FAITH, GIANT CONFIDENCE IN GOD, GIANT ABILITY TO LEAD AND LIVE FROM THE WELL OF FAVOR AND ABUNDANCE.

This kind of living is not without trouble, but it is victorious living.

WEEK 12

Excellence

Always, always strive for excellence. Make excellence your calling card. It should never matter whether you like what you are doing. Become so committed to excellence in what you do that it becomes second nature, as if it were ingrained into your DNA. Excellence breeds opportunities. It is the fertilizer in the soil of success.

Thought:

Promotion has a season of preparation attached to it. If one is promoted too soon, there is a greater chance of failure and self-destruction.

Colossians 3:23 (KJVS) states, "And whatsoever ye do, do it heartily as to the Lord, and not unto men." The Amplified Bible captures this instruction a little more clearly, "Whatever may be your task, work at it heartily (from the soul), as [something done] for the Lord and not for men." This is the way I try to live my life. Protect the business and assets of others as if they were God's.

Doing this will reinforce and uphold your desire to serve with excellence. God is ultimately where all promotion comes from. Therefore, always see yourself as working for the best boss there is...God.

WEEK 13

Greatness is Cultivated!

Greatness is like a beautiful garden. It does not come into existence by natural progression. A beautiful garden requires sunlight, irrigation, and the proper fertilizer for the best yield of fruits and vegetables at the expected harvest time. Greatness is no different. A garden can have great soil. However, if it is not properly irrigated, it will not produce at the desired level. In this same manner, doing nothing is not the way to sustain the greatness of one's gifts. Gifts must be nurtured. Gifts require practice and expert guidance to be mastered so that they may yield the highest possible return, which is excellence. The gift that has been nurtured to excellence will determine your compensation and, thereby, your greatness!

Apostle Paul speaks about planting the Word into people's lives in 1 Corinthians 3 when he says, "I have planted, Apollos watered, but God gave the increase." Ultimately, God is responsible for the outcome. It is our job to plant and water as we disciple others. Did Moses not "plant" and "water" Joshua? Did Elijah not do the same with Elisha? When great people mentor and pour their lives into others, it allows generational greatness to happen. Planting and watering transfer the calling into a mantle that can be passed on to a successor. God expects us to have a succession plan. Therefore, we must be about the business of cultivating and growing the abilities of others. The wisdom and expertise we have are valuable and meant to be shared. Whatever your gift and area of expertise, start looking for opportunities to pour into the lives of others in your current circle of activity. You will be amazed at people's positive response to your offer to help them learn, improve, and add something valuable to their lives.

WEEK 14

Seek Strength from the Inside Out

Inner strength is that immeasurable force that propels us. It is the spirit inside us that guides us. When the spirit of a person is fed with words of faith that produce the right kind of thinking, that person grows in wisdom, strength, and the ability to believe. They flourish from the inside out as they step into the world and strive toward their destiny.

Thought:

If you start measuring your success by the number of other people you help to succeed, it will not only change your perspective. It will change your heart.

Paul spoke of what he prayed for the church at Ephesus and in Ephesians 3:14-19 he states, "For this cause I bow my knees unto the Father of our Lord Jesus Christ, of whom the whole family in heaven and earth is named. That he would grant you according to the riches of his glory, to be strengthened with might by his Spirit in the inner man; that Christ may dwell in your hearts by faith; that ye; be rooted and grounded in love, may be able to comprehend with all saints what is the breath, and length, and depth and height; And to know the love of Christ, which passeth knowledge, that ye might be filled with all the fullness of God."

It is the inner man's strength that gives us the ability to boldly go at our assignment with the understanding that God is going to use everything to bring out the best in us. He has a plan for us that is better than anything we have imagined. He loves us and knows what is best for us. Paul's prayer was for the success of the church at Ephesus. He wanted the people there to live successfully through their relationship with God

WEEK 15

Problems, Troubles, Destruction

What do you do when the world around you seem to be falling apart? What is the wisdom when a plan comes apart at the seams? First, give yourself a little time to grieve and reflect on disappointments or failures (only a little time) and learn from any mistakes. Second, limit the time you take to grieve and set a specific point when you will get back to action. Move methodically and deliberately back into action. Third, if you have a trustworthy, wise network of people around you, ask for their opinions and counsel as you move forward. Finally, do not give up before your breakthrough. You must continue to keep your mind focused on your ultimate success and have a clear understanding of the challenges you face.

Thought:

Imperfection and past failures do not disqualify you from future success. Submitting to fear and believing in negative circumstances are the real disqualifiers

Second Corinthians 4:8-11 reminds us that to live this life successfully requires perseverance. Paul says, "We are troubled on every side, yet not distressed; we are perplexed, but not in despair; persecuted, but not forsaken; cast down, but not destroyed. Always bearing about in the body the dying of the Lord Jesus, that the life also of Jesus might be made manifest in our body.

Wow! We endure with perseverance and faith, allowing Christ to live through us. We also achieve victory through perseverance. God is on our side, and we win by never quitting.

WEEK 16

What Is Causing You to Wait?

Is it fear? Identify the things you are afraid of. Is it a lack of confidence? Identify the things that make you doubt yourself. Is it a lack of resources? Get specific about your financial needs and create a plan that will help you launch your dream opportunity. When you reflect on pursuing your dream and launching into the unknown, don't dwell on the things that give you a nervous or upset stomach. Write down the things that stagnate you—the things you use as excuses and reasons not to step out and take a shot at your dream. You will find that some of the reasons you give are legitimate, but others are not. Start to create a plan to address the real concerns, but also understand and accept that you will not have all the answers and will not eliminate all the risks. The most important question to ask yourself is: are your fears, lack of confidence, or lack of resources worth not trying to live the dream you have for your life? If the answer is no, wake up, get up, and start marching toward your destiny!

Hebrews 10:35 (KJVS) states, "Cast not away your confidence, which hath great recompense of reward." There is a reward attached to confidence. Romans 4:20 speaks of Abraham being "strong in faith" and "fully persuaded" that God was able to perform what He had promised. That sounds a lot like complete confidence to me. 2 Timothy 1:7 informs us that fear is not from God; He gives us power, love, and a sound mind. You can use these scriptures to remind yourself where God stands. Will strengthening my inner man help me walk in power? Will it help me walk in love? Will strengthening my inner man and my use of godly wisdom and good judgment further my efforts to walk in a sound mind? These are important questions, and the correct answers will help you remove fear and doubt.

WEEK 17

The Power of Pain

Pain is physical, psychological, or emotional suffering. It is a force that can alter the path of a person's life. Pain can take people to strange places if it is allowed to take over the driver's seat of life. It can also be a catalyst and an agent of irrational thinking. Pain is the usual suspect responsible for self-destructive behaviors. Yet, if one correctly understands pain and its power, they will move to harness it in such a way that it propels them towards their destiny. Identifying how pain impacts your behavior and renewing your thinking so you can purposely change your response to pain are important abilities and requirements. Once you understand this requirement, pain can become a great teacher, allowing you to stop repeatedly making mistakes. Repetitive mistakes steal valuable time away from reaching and living your destiny. The pain of poverty can propel someone towards wealth. The pain of isolation and alienation can lead a person to understand how to teach others to live in harmony with each other. The pain of abuse can drive someone to create a place to protect others. Pain is something that few of us desire to experience, yet some of the best things in life have their roots in pain.

John 11:35, "Jesus wept," is often referred to as the shortest verse in the Bible. Chapter 11 speaks of the events surrounding the death of Lazarus. The death of Lazarus was a painful event for Jesus, but it was also a display of the full expression of God at work. In John 11:24-26 (KJV), Martha said, "I know that he (Lazarus) shall rise again in the resurrection at the last day." Jesus replied, "I am the resurrection, and the life; he that believeth in me, though he were dead, yet shall he live: And whosoever liveth and believeth in me shall never die." Jesus was saying we don't have to wait until the last day—I am the walking embodiment of resurrection power! After Jesus prayed and thanked the Father, He loudly said, "Lazarus, come forth." The man who had been dead for four days came forth… alive and well. Pain is often the catalyst for absolute proof of God's power!

WEEK 18

Teacher! Teacher!

Who is your teacher today? Is it someone who simply will not cooperate with your plan? Is it someone who resists every good goal and objective you have? Is it a glass ceiling acting as a barrier between you and your potential? At this very moment, who or what do you have the opportunity to learn from? I challenge you to rename all your "obstacles." Rename every obstacle as your "teacher." Do it today! Change your outlook and focus on what you can learn—both about the "teacher" and how the "teacher" impacts you.

You can listen and learn. You can experience and learn. The most important thing is to LEARN. Once you have learned, teach others. Teaching others the life lessons you have learned is a sign of maturity. Teaching is a type of servanthood. Hebrews 5:12 (KJVS) says, "For when for the time ye ought to be teachers, ye have need that one teach you again which be the first principles of the oracles of God; and are become such as have need of milk, and not of strong meat." Second Timothy 2:24 (KJVS) says, "And the servant of the Lord must not strive; but be gentle unto all men; apt to teach, patient." Look to those who walk in maturity. Look to those who are patient and willing to share their wisdom and understanding.

WEEK 19

Money and the Fuse

Built into each one of us is the power to bring wealth into our lives through our gift when coupled with faith and obedience to the proper principles. Our gift can be a talent. It can show itself as an acumen, propensity, or passion to see, develop, and understand something beyond the norm. When the right opportunities meet our inherent gifts, talents, acumen, propensity, or passion, it is often like lighting a stick of dynamite. The fuse burns down to an end, then explodes and propels us to a position of wealth. The fuse can be very short, or it can be very long. Overnight success is rarely overnight. My mother would often say, "Overnight success takes 15 years." You must understand that when a fuse has been lit, you must protect it and be careful to let nothing and no one put it out before you blow up!

Most importantly, you must know where the power to earn originates. Deuteronomy 8:18 (NIV) states, "But remember the Lord your God, for it is He who gives you the ability to produce wealth, and so confirms His covenant, which He swore to your ancestors, as it is today." God is the foundation of every believer's success. He causes all things to work together for our good. He can use disappointment or failure to teach us how to triumph. He is the author of all promotion that comes into our lives. In living our success, we must remember that we are also heirs to God's established covenant. Any money we have really belongs to Him. That is why we give to the causes that God directs us to give to. God puts money into our hands to do His good will on this earth.

In the area of finances, the scripture that has been the most impactful in my life is 2 Corinthians 9:8-10 (AMP), which states, "And God is able to make all grace (every favor and earthly blessing) come to you in abundance, so that you may always and under all circumstances and whatever the need, be self-sufficient [possessing enough to require no aid or support and furnished in abundance for every good work and charitable donation]. As it is written, he [the benevolent person] scatters abroad; he gives to the poor. His deeds of justice, goodness, kindness, and benevolence will go on forever. And [God] who provides seed for the sower and bread for the eating will also multiply your [resources for] sowing and increase the fruits of your righteousness [which manifests itself in active goodness, kindness, and charity]."

Every time I read these passages, the words prick my heart and penetrate my spirit. Reading it is an emotional experience for me because the Word in this area has been real in my life. I want this Word to continue to grow in me. I want to be a blessing to the people I encounter. Start wherever you are and bless someone else in some way every week. Purposefully do something good for someone else every week without any expectation of a returned favor. If you do this for a year, it will be so deeply entrenched in your DNA that you will continue it for a lifetime. God will begin to multiply the good that you do.

WEEK 20

Celebrate Current Success and the Future at the Same Time

People often say that we should take the time to celebrate our successes. This is very true. Yes, we should pause and express happiness and gratitude to those who helped us accomplish a great goal. Celebrating successes represents important opportunities to present a brief outline of plans beyond the current success. This is the time to express confidence in the team and their work. It is also a good time to make sure that belief and faith remain ignited. Successes are foundational. Each one is like laying another floor on a planned skyscraper. Successes are also like battles in a war. Each battle won brings you closer to the final victory you seek. When you talk about the successes of a team, its leaders use those successes to build faith and trust. Leaders make sure they communicate a clear vision of how the current success plays into their long-range goals.

The previous paragraph points out the

importance of applying faith to leadership, no matter the discipline. Yet to be able to do this, there is something you must have deep inside yourself. It is seen in two scriptural principles needed to lead.The first principle is found in 2 Corin- thians 5:7 (AMP), "For we walk by faith [we regulate our lives and conduct ourselves by our convictions or beliefs regarding man's relationship to God and divine things, with trust and holy fervor; thus, we walk] not by sight or appearance." The second principle is found in Proverbs 4:7 (AMP) which tells us to get wisdom (skillful and godly wisdom)! because skillful and godly wisdom are the principal things. And with all you have gotten, also get understanding (discernment, comprehension and inter- pretation). The combination of faith and wisdom is critical for successful leadership. Faith is needed to have the vision and the active belief required to guide yourself and others. Wisdom comes from hearing God's instruction during the time you spend with Him and through the wise counsel of those you surround yourself with.

If you keep faith and wisdom at the forefront of all that you do, you can build that skyscraper of success layer by layer, floor by floor.

WEEK 21

Sumthin' in the Milk Ain't Clean

Sumthin' in the milk ain't clean is an expression my grandmother affectionately used when there was something or someone amid an important goal deliberately making things go wrong. Sometimes, you must pause in the middle of activities to find out where the poison is before it kills what you are trying to achieve. It is the equivalent of running a 26-mile marathon over rugged terrain and getting bitten by a rattlesnake 13 miles in. There is no way you can keep going. You must stop and deal with the deadly poison, or you won't ever be racing again. At least, it won't be in this world. You must evaluate the level of toxicity to know whether it is one that requires you to stop. If it requires a stop, stop! Extract the poison and begin to move forward again.

Thought:

Winning must be rooted in righteousness. Cheating to win is a result of pride and arrogance, showing that you feel entitled to something you are unwilling to earn through honest work.

The scripture that comes to mind is one my grandmother, whom we affectionately called "Nana," would often quote. Nana would often say, "Meditate on Psalm 37 if someone is doing you wrong." Psalm 37:1-5 (KJVS) says, "Fret not thyself because of evildoers, neither be thou envious against the workers of iniquity. For they shall soon be cut down like the grass and wither as the green herb. Trust in the Lord and do good, so shalt thou dwell in the land and verily thou shalt be fed. Delight thyself also in the Lord; and he shall give thee the desires of thine heart. Commit thy way unto the Lord; trust also in him; and he shall bring it to pass."

There are times when the snake along your life's journey is someone you did not expect it to be. When that happens, increase your commitment of your time and talents to the Lord, and you will see His goodness in the land of the living, and your enemies will flee in seven different directions!

WEEK 22

Wake Up Every Day and Decide How You Want to Live

One of the greatest gifts given to us as human beings is the ability to choose. If we wake up every day and make high-quality decisions, it will not be hard to ultimately live a high-quality life. Regularly making high-quality decisions will have a profound effect on your life. The problem is that we often lose sight of the fact that we must make important decisions daily. Eating right and exercising provide clear examples. You can't make the decision to eat right or exercise once and receive the benefit of good health. You must make a good health decision every time you have a food proposition. You must decide over and over again to push yourself and commit to a certain number of days to exercise each week. It is no different from deciding to save $100 every pay period. You must resist temptations that will keep you from sustaining that commitment. You will need to make the choice to resist temptations again and again.

Strength and power are the result of making high quality decisions over and over again.

Joshua 24:14-15 says, "Now therefore fear the Lord and serve him in sincerity and in truth; and put away the gods which your fathers served on the other side of the flood, and in Egypt and serve ye the Lord. And if it seems evil unto you to serve the Lord, choose you this day whom ye will serve, whether the gods which your fathers served that were on the other side of the flood, or the gods of the Amorites, in whose land ye dwell: but as for me and my house, we will serve the Lord. And the people answered and said, God forbid that we should forsake the Lord to serve other gods."

Decisions about doing right must be committed to again and again. Why? You are walking around in a body. Your body can only function in righteousness if your spirit man is in control of that body and if your spirit is in submission to the Holy Spirit. This fallen world will constantly test your flesh. You must choose, again and again, not to give place to evil.

WEEK 23

The Power of Believing in What You Do Not See

The seen realm is what it is. The key to designing a path to your destiny is understanding that believing is seeing and not the other way around. Believing is at the heart and core of who you are. Believing is designed by God to function as sight. You may not see every detail with physical eyesight, but believing will be a light to your path. It will become a guiding light that provides the necessary sense of direction. Believing will push you to knock on doors that you would not normally knock on. It will cause you to find answers to questions in places you least expect to find them. Believing will take you out of your comfort zone and beyond the borders that have been around your life.

You must work on seeing with your heart and spirit. This kind of seeing requires us to remove doubt. Mark 11:23- 24 (NIV) says, "Truly I tell you, if anyone says to this mountain, Go throw yourself into the sea, and does not doubt in their heart but believes that what they say will happen, it will be done for them." Doubt at the heart level can keep you from experiencing the vision God has given you for your life. Go after, remove, and obliterate the doubt that is trying to keep you in a box.

Thought:

Work diligently to turn off the noise in your life so that you can focus on the activities that drive you towards your destiny.

WEEK 24

The Value of Self Diagnostics

There is major power in being able to correct yourself—the power of self-analysis of your motives, actions, and biases. There should be an entire list that you check off before finalizing your decisions. Are you able to question yourself in such a way that you can find the flaw that is leading to bad decisions? A self-diagnosis may show that you are rushing to judgment without all the facts. Self-diagnosis can show that your feelings about a person are affecting your ability to listen to them or hear their ideas. When you can examine yourself and root out your own toxic thinking, you will become a master decision-maker.

Thought:

You cannot legislate policy that involves issues of the heart. You must touch people directly to change a heart issue.

The more time you spend building and maintaining your spirit man, the more disciplined you will become about self-correction.

In 2 Timothy 3:16-17 (KJVS) Paul writes, "All scripture is given by inspiration of God, and is profitable for doctrine, for reproof, for correction, for instruction in righteousness: that the man of God may be perfect, thoroughly furnished unto all good works." We must have the right thing inside us to have the ability to self-correct. There is no better way to learn self-correction than by spending time in God's Word.

WEEK 25

Nutrition for the Inner Man

The food of God's Word and the strength training of faith must be where they need to be for the inner man to continue growing. As the physical body needs good food and exercise for longevity, the spirit of a man (the inner man) has a similar and even greater need. If you are being nourished by word food and teachings that do not provide enough nutrition for your stage of growth, it can cause inner man malnutrition. The nutrition must fit the stage of growth you are in and the stage you are moving toward.

Thought:

Attitudes and perceptions can change when new evidence is presented. However, the ultimate truth does not change. It exists and waits to be discovered.

When the woman with the issue of blood touched Jesus' garment and was healed, in Luke 17:19, Jesus said to her, "Thy faith hath made thee whole." It is the feeding and nurturing of our faith that makes the inner man strong. Faith is fed through the ears and not through the mouth. Romans 10:17 states, "So then faith cometh by hearing, and hearing by the Word of God." Regularly hearing the Word of God strengthens faith. The present tense of the word "hearing" positions it as something to be continually done. Your faith stays strong by consistent exposure to God's Word.

WEEK 26

Write Your Own Book!

You may have failed, flunked, and bombed out! Yet, that is not the end of your story. In fact, it is often the beginning of a new chapter. Learning from mistakes and bad experiences makes you stronger, wiser, and often a great teacher to others. Use the experiences you've had to first lead yourself to success. Then, teach and lead others to their success. If you are breathing, this is your life's mission. Your life lessons have tremendous value.

Thought:

Most worthy challenges are infused with the word "and", like "winning and doing the right thing."

Ephesians 6 (KJVS) speaks of us putting on the whole armor of God to fight spiritual wickedness. There are a bunch of "ands" in these scriptural verses. You are going to need more than one thing to win the fight against spiritual wickedness. "Having your loins girt about with truth and having on the breastplate of righteousness."

"And take the helmet of salvation and the sword of the Spirit, which is the Word of God" There is power in understanding the importance of "and."

WEEK 27

Stop Lying to Yourself!

People who lie to themselves end up living at a level that is beneath their destiny. They constantly justify actions that keep them stuck. They will not follow the advice of people who love them and care about their well-being. They often won't follow the advice of experts in the area where they need help. They reject all attempts to help them because of pride or embarrassment. They focus all their energy on the things they are good at and ignore the things that have not produced success. All the while, these things are more powerful than their good actions and keep them stuck. Listen, do not be this person. Push yourself to have a spirit that is teachable. Open yourself up to constructive criticism that will allow you to improve. All growth takes root in being honest with yourself.

According to John 8:32 (AMP), "the truth will set you free." Truth sets guardrails. When you go outside of the truth, you create a false image of who you really are. The longer you live a lie, the more lies you become comfortable hearing and living with. Proverbs 17:4 (AMP) says, "An evildoer gives heed to wicked lips; and a liar listens to a mischievous tongue." The truth can lead to breakthroughs in things that held you back. When the truth is known and acted upon, freedom is at hand.

WEEK 28

Dark Temptations

Dark temptations are those things that you desire but are not good for you. The things that are damaging to your focus. The things that you know are not right for you, but you have a strong desire to consistently have the experience related to that dark temptation anyway.

The first thing needed to win is to acknowledge that the dark temptation is wrong for you and that it is a weakness. Second, try not to fight against the temptation alone. Connect with just one person whom you trust completely to walk through your thinking with and ask him or her to help you be accountable for your actions. This needs to be someone you can always be totally honest with—someone who will keep the information you have shared to himself or herself.

Third, avoid putting yourself in situations that would make you more vulnerable. Giving in to our weaknesses can destroy lives, careers, and golden opportunities. You may never be strong in this area, but it is critical to control your weaknesses.

In week 9, Apostle Paul talked about evil always being present when we are trying to do good. James 4:7 tells us, "Submit yourselves therefore to God. Resist the devil, and he will flee from you." Resisting requires us to draw near to God and create boundaries for ourselves—boundaries and accountability on the straight and narrow path. It is wise to have someone in your life who can provide Spirit-filled insight and act as an accountability partner. This person must have wisdom so that he or she can provide what you need.

WEEK 29

Be Ready for the Ordained Moment That Will Lead to Your Success

Is it an elevator pitch for your idea? Is it a business plan? Is it training that you need? Is it about improving your public speaking skills? How do you prepare yourself for the ordained moment with the person who can cause your dream opportunity to manifest? Preparation is the proof of your expectation and the evidence of your faith. If you believe it will happen, you will prepare for it to happen!

Thought:

Show people your heart through your actions.

1 Peter 3:15 (KJVS) the scripture says, "But sanctify the Lord in your hearts: and be ready always to give every man that asketh you a reason for the hope that is in you with meekness and fear."

If God wants us to always be ready to answer

every man about our hopes, how do we not apply this same principle to our own calling? Our calling is something that God wants us to do. God wants us to value being prepared to take on the calling. Hebrews 13:20-21 (NIV) states, "Now may the God of peace, who through the blood of the eternal covenant brought back from the dead our Lord Jesus, that great Shepherd of the sheep, equip you with everything good for doing his will." God wants us and puts us in situations that prepare us to fulfill His calling. Let us stand ready at every moment!

WEEK 30

Dog Eat Ya' Share

It is a phrase my grandmother used to denote missed opportunities. I believe she meant it this way: If you don't work on capitalizing on the opportunities presented, the dogs—or the masses of people who want their share and everyone else's—will consume the success that was supposed to come to you through those missed opportunities. That is why all sensible and reasonable opportunities must be explored. Each opportunity should be evaluated for its worth. Success is the culmination of wisely selected and activated opportunities.

Thought:

Leverage the things you are gifted at. Your gifts speak to power and expand your influence.

Proverbs 18:16 (KJVS) says, "A man's gift maketh room for him, and bringeth him before great men." Never let the gift that God has placed in you become dormant. You must keep your gift sharp and active.

WEEK 31

The Architect of Your World

When you know your destiny, when you know what has been placed inside of you, train your thoughts, temper your words, and purpose your actions to line up with what you know. Let those thoughts, words, and actions become your drafting pencil. Use those tools to fulfill the destiny that has been placed inside of you. Your thoughts will be the beginning of the house you will build — the legacy that you will put in place for your family. Be generations-minded.

Thought:

Fear shrinks your possibilities and courage expands them. When you believe this truth, the choice is easy!

Genesis 1:26 (KJVS) says, "And God said, let us make man in our image, after our likeness: and let them have dominion over the fish of the sea, and over the fowl of the air, and over the cattle, and over all the earth, and over every creeping thing that creeps upon the earth."

Originally, God placed man in a position of authority. That was how we were designed. When we operate in submission to God's precepts, as the two servants in the parable of the talents did, God restores us to a position of leadership [dominion]. We are given back the authority we **lost** to the devil through Adam's disobedience. When authority is placed in the hands of a righteous man or woman, the world functions as God has designed it. This is done, first and foremost, in love. Love is the ultimate governing force.

WEEK 32

Stop Worrying About All the Things That Might Go Wrong!

You must fight against spending your time thinking only about the things that can go wrong. This is not to say you should not be prepared for things not going as planned. You should have a contingency or alternative plan for everything that could happen, including the bad things. Most of your focus should be on the strategic execution needed to have a successful outcome. This holds true for your personal life as well. You must focus most of your energy on the GOOD and living a life that helps the GOOD expand.

Thought:

Everything you value should be tempered with wisdom and understanding. Deciding on the risks you undertake, the partnerships you form, the investments you make, and even the spouse you choose should be guided by wisdom. Wisdom and understanding are foundational to attaining and sustaining a well-lived life.

Matthew 6:33-34 (AMP) states, "But seek (aim at and strive after) first His kingdom and His righteousness (His way of doing and being right), and then all these things taken together will be given you besides. So do not worry or be anxious about tomorrow, for tomorrow will have worries and anxieties of its own. Sufficient for each day is its own trouble." Focusing on God allows Him to guide us along a path that keeps us in righteousness and in a place where our needs will be met. That is God's aim!

WEEK 33

Using Up Precious Personal Energy Arguing with Others

Make an effort to avoid arguing about insignificant things that amount to nothing in the grand scheme of things. They consume energy and brainpower that should be focused on the important personal and professional goals you are trying to accomplish. Arguing about insignificant things can be divisive and cause a rift between you and important members of your team. Instead, view differences as assets that help drive better decision-making. Use differences to consider perspectives you would not ordinarily acknowledge and to widen your understanding of those around you. Educate yourself on the perspectives that others hold and the reasons behind them. Over time, this will help you make more successful decisions.

Romans chapter 14 gives us wise instruction about having arguments around disputable matters. Romans 14:5 (NIV) says, "One person considers one day more sacred than another; another considers every day alike.

Each of them should be fully convinced in their own mind." Romans 14 admonishes us about not judging one another over minor differences in our understanding of the Word. This is the way to temper all minor disputes.

WEEK 34

Learn to Find Comfort in Your Discomfort

Things that cause you to be uncomfortable are not always bad. In fact, they often present opportunities to grow. If you can get past the anxiety and fear, you can start thinking about the discomfort from the perspective of finding a solution. You can start thinking about the discomfort strategically. You can also learn about yourself by analyzing how the discomfort initially made you feel. You can learn how to control your reactions and think through your initial response. With this understanding, you can learn how to lead yourself and others through rough seas. Your faith will help you get through the storms.

Ananias was clearly uncomfortable when Jesus spoke to him about going to Saul so that he might receive his sight. Ananias reminded Jesus of "how much evil he [Saul] hath done to thy saints at Jerusalem." Nevertheless, Ananias obeyed Jesus despite his personal discomfort. Saul, whose name was later changed to Paul, ended up writing most of the New Testament and gave us a rich revelation of our new covenant in Jesus Christ. As Jesus said, Paul was a chosen vessel.

Sometimes, God gives us tasks that are very uncomfortable to do. Yet, these are the tasks that allow us to go far beyond our best expectations. These God-given tasks help to make our spirit man strong. They fortify our trust in God

WEEK 35

Face a Fight Head On, Never Cut and Run!

Problems are never solved by running away. Courage is not moving forward in the absence of fear; it is moving forward despite fear. Courage means trusting and having faith in the nurtured gifts that have built up your inner man. Courage is having enough trust to launch out into the unknown. It is a power. It is a fire. Courage is the thing inside us that makes us fight through fear. Winning takes us beyond borders and boundaries; it takes us to our destiny. The very thing that was in our heart, which we originally thought was impossible, is often on the other side of a problem or obstacle you are facing. This is where victory lives.

Thought:

Life is hard, but victorious living can make the challenges sweet. Victories are manifestations of successful living that increase our faith.

In 1 Kings 18 Elijah takes on Ahab, Jezebel and the prophets of Baal. If you are familiar with the story, you know that the prophets cried aloud and cut themselves, trying to get Baal to answer by fire, but it never happened for them. Elijah poured water over the sacrificial bullock and the wood to make certain that there would be no reason to doubt God. Elijah said, "Lord God of Abraham, Isaac, and of Israel, let it be known this day that thou art God in Israel and that I am thy servant, and that I have done all these things at thy word."

The fire of the Lord fell and consumed the sacrificial bullock, the wood, the stones, the dust, and licked up the water in the trench around the altar. Elijah told the people to take the prophets of Baal and let not one of them get away. Elijah slew the prophets of Baal. Once Jezebel knew about the prophets of Baal being slain, she sent word to Elijah that she was going to have him killed. To escape Jezebel's wrath, Elijah then fled for his life.

The amazing thing is that Elijah was tuned in to God – so much so that he was able to have God answer by fire. Yet, immediately following this display of God's power, Elijah ran from Jezebel.

Could Elijah have stood his ground and **taken** Jezebel head-on? Maybe. Yet, God knows our frame. He knows what we are made of. Moses argued with God about not being a good public speaker, and God ended up letting Aaron speak on Moses' behalf, even though He told Moses He would tell him what to say.

When we understand the power of God, we know how to react in every situation. God wants us to remove both doubt in Him and self-doubt.

WEEK 36

Dwell in the Place of Growth

Your dreams are like a garden that must be properly maintained in order to grow well. Your focus should be on those who also help you grow. Leave behind the places and people of stagnation. Leave the places that lack nourishment. Leave the places that do not edify your inner self. Leave the things that try to return you to a barren place. Keep the words! Keep the vision! Keep the people, places, and things in your heart, in your view, and on your mind that keep you on track to the destiny designed for you! Fertilize your dream!

Isaiah 58: (KJVS) says, "And the Lord shall guide thee continually and satisfy thy soul in drought and make fat thy bones: and thou shalt be like a watered garden, and like a spring of water whose waters fail not."

Following God always takes us to a place of growth, maturity, strength, and understanding. These are the places where we are truly designed to flourish.

WEEK 37

Look for New Ways to Inspire Yourself

You may need to stay focused on a goal or project for quite a long time to see its success manifest. The important thing that you must learn is how to continually and creatively inspire yourself. Staying motivated despite the challenges requires consistent deposits of faith-filled words into your spirit. These deposits must be stronger than your natural reasoning. Your desire to live out your calling must be stronger than your belief in circumstantial opposition. You must stay active with both big and small things that support the calling on your life.

Romans 15:4 (NIV) states, "For everything that was written in the past was written to teach us, so that through the endurance taught in the Scriptures and the encouragement they provide we might have hope." Throughout the Scriptures, stories teach us about endurance. Many stories of endurance are found in the lives of other believers around you. Our staying encouraged and active depends on staying tuned into God and godly people who are walking in their own calling.

WEEK 38

Wisdom & Self-Control

Wisdom and self-control are spiritual keys to unlocking many of the natural manifestations of goodness in this gift known as the human experience. Wisdom opens us up to revelations. Wisdom helps us capture the moments that matter — moments that elevate our experiences and strengthen us for our journey. Wisdom is necessary to succeed in our daily lives. Self-control keeps us from being derailed or sidetracked by things of little value. Self-control helps us prioritize. So, be ready and go when the right moments appear.

Thought:

Sacrifice is the "work part" of both love and leadership.

Self-control is one of the fruits of the Spirit of God. It helps you stay within the will of God. It is a source of that inner man strength that keeps the deceiver out of your life. Galatians 5:24 (NIV) talks about people who exhibit self-control stating, "Those who belong to Christ Jesus have crucified the flesh with its passions and desires. Since, we live by the Spirit, let us keep in step with the Spirit."

WEEK 39

The Essence of Your Destiny

Maturity and courage are required to create the future you are destined for. Maturity requires us to stop living with selfish thoughts and desires of the moment. Maturity and courage drive us to plan, design, and take calculated risks that advance our destiny. You must want your destiny more than the smaller and ultimately unsatisfying distractions that entangle us moment by moment. As we untie the ropes of those distractions, our vision and purpose become clear.

James 3:16 (NIV) says, "For where you have envy and selfish ambition, there you find disorder and every evil practice." Selfishness brings evil along with it because it makes people feel entitled to what they have no right to possess." Mark 8:34 (NIV) says, "Whoever wants to be my disciple must deny themselves and take up their cross and follow me." The power to deny self requires maturity and maturity requires studying and an understanding of God's precepts.

WEEK 40

Put Away Childish Things to Avoid Loss

Childish things only delay us from living in the fullness of our destiny. There is power in self-control and understanding the payoff of personal discipline. We must stay tuned to the things that help us maintain our willpower and strength as we move towards our destiny. We tend to sink into undisciplined and childish behavior when we are weak. We must avoid and remove people and things that weaken our efforts.

As believers, many of us are aware of 1 Corinthians 13:11 (KJVS) which says, "When I was a child, I spake as a child, I understood as a child, I thought as a child; but when I became a man, I put away childish things." Often, a slow start to life and not becoming mature until later in life impacts people in profound ways. Instead of buying your first house at 30 years of age, you are doing it at 40. You played too much and behaved immaturely 10 years longer than you should have. We put away childish things to get moving on our calling. Our calling requires commitment, diligence, discipline and focus. It is hard to play and work on your calling at the same time. You should set aside time for rest, relaxation and fun but do not let it occupy the core of your activities. Your mission and calling should represent that core, always.

WEEK 41

The Creator's Nature

As human beings, we are the greatest creation walking the face of the earth. From the creativity that birthed us, we were impregnated with our own abundant creativity! The creation of planes, trains, automobiles, computers, software, broadband, and every imaginable device — what will we do next? That is up to you. Energize your creativity. Don't let it be dormant. Fuel your creative juices by making time for thinking and brainstorming. Fuel creativity by surrounding yourself with people who are both creative and detail-oriented. That way, you can take an idea through all its phases.

We are made in God's image and likeness. God is the source of our creativity. When God breathed the breath of life into Adam's nostrils, the living soul that went into man was God's creativity. Genesis 11:5-6 (KJVS) tells us, "And the Lord came down to see the city and the tower, which the children of men built. And the Lord said, behold the people is one, they all have one language; and this they begin to do; and now nothing will be restrained from them, which they have imagined to do."

When people are unified, their power is magnified and maximized. For this reason, it is important for your heart to be in the right place. Power in the hands of those with the right heart can achieve great things for God and make the world a better place.

WEEK 42

What Defines Your World?

What is your world like? Who defines it? Who dictates where the boundaries and limits are? Who determines its direction? Who calls the shots? Never covet the things that you do not own or control. Focus on developing the creativity needed to build on what you already possess. Use your gifts and relationships, rooted in integrity, to build the resources you need to launch your ship into deep seas and move yourself toward your destiny. As you cross the seas, you will find that you have more than enough to reach successes that exceed your every expectation. Stop looking at what you do not have and focus on working with what you do have. Your success is imminent!

In 2 Kings 4, Elisha was helping a widow whose two sons were about to be taken as bondsmen to cover an unpaid debt. Elisha asked the widow, "What hast thou in the house? And she said, "Thine handmaid hath not anything in the house, save a pot of oil."

At Elisha's instruction, the woman poured oil into many different vessels until she had poured enough to pay off her debt and still had oil left. She had no idea that God would take that one pot of oil and multiply it to meet the need she had and more.

This scripture taught me to ask myself, "What do I have in my own hands?" What resource do I have right now that I can use to better my situation? The solution to your problem, condition or circumstance might be at your fingertips. There may be something that you already possess that God can do something miraculous with.

WEEK 43

Let Your Light Shine!

Many good-natured people believe in putting their heads down and working hard. These good-natured people work with excellence, and they don't worry about who gets the credit. In fact, they avoid the spotlight as if it were a virus. However, I want to encourage those of you who quietly work in excellence to come out of the shadows and display your true selves. Your light was never meant to be hidden; instead, it should be displayed openly and brighten any space where you are. Shells are hard to come out of, but these comfort zones can keep you and others from their destinies. The example you set is meant to inspire others. You don't have to be charismatic to lead. The most important characteristic of leadership is courage.

In Matthew 5:14-16 (KJVS) Jesus says, "Ye are the light of the world. A city that is set on a hill cannot be hid. Neither do men light a candle and put it under a bushel basket, but on a candlestick; and it giveth light unto all that are in the house. Let your light so shine before men, that they might see your good works, and glorify your Father which is in heaven."

You certainly should not brag about the good you do but you also should not hide it. Let your life and the actions you take speak for who you truly are. Your daily actions should speak to who you are at your core. The person that God designed you to be.

WEEK 44

Let's Fly!

When it is time to fly, you must get on the plane and go! Great opportunities are like flights to unknown destinations. You may get on the plane not knowing where the destination is, but ultimately, it will be somewhere good. Remember, your destiny can be a journey of significant distance. You may need to take several connecting flights to get there. You will go up and sometimes come down. The times when you are down must be used for fueling your journey with knowledge, wise counsel, and continued self-development. You must become masterful at using your time wisely. These things will enlarge your impact and influence.

Thought:

Wisdom requires courage and faith is the fuel that courage needs.

To live a life where you soar means living life by faith. Faith is the framework of the impossible. Abraham, the father of faith, "staggered not at the promise of God through unbelief; but was strong in faith, giving glory to God; and being fully persuaded that what He had promised, he was able to perform" according to Romans 4:20- 21.

In Genesis 17:17, we learn that Abraham was around 100 years old and his wife Sarah was around 90 years old at the time God promised them a son. At first, Abraham laughed but God's Word did not change. Over time, Abraham became fully persuaded that God's words were the truth no matter what the circumstances were. Let's all fly by truly believing that the impossible is possible with God.

WEEK 45

Fight like a Soldier, with Conviction, and to the Death if Necessary

A willingness to go harder and longer than anyone else is a differentiator. Most people give up before their breakthrough. The battle over who wants it most is always wrapped in persevering. Perseverance is the refusal to give up or give in. It is a powerful force. Be a person who uses the powerful force of perseverance!

Thought:

Truth is a powerful agent of change. Truth challenges but also empowers leaders to steer their teams through turbulent waters onward to victory.

The truth is a weapon that you can fight with and win. When we go to a battle with the proper weapons, truth and righteousness should be among them. Christ was willing to fight sin and death by giving up his own life. God gave us victory over sin and death through our Lord Jesus Christ. Galatians 3:13 (KJVS) says, "Christ has redeemed us from the curse of the law, being made a curse for us." He had to pay a price to purchase our lives and, through Him, place us in a position of victory. His victory required persevering punishment.

WEEK 46

Kill That Noise!

I can't emphasize enough the importance of staying the course. Allowing distractions to occur leads to dissatisfaction. Perseverance is good, but perseverance with focus is best. It is the combination of these two qualities that leads to sustained, successful living.

I used to often say "DDF" to my son. DDF was my constant reminder of three important traits my son needed in order to be successful in his schoolwork and in life. The traits are DISCIPLINE, DILIGENCE, and FOCUS. There will always be things that distract you. Someone or something will find "stuff" to steal your energy and your time.

In Proverbs 10:4 (KJVS) King Solomon said, "He becometh poor that dealeth with a slack hand: but the hand of the diligent maketh rich."

When you wrap diligence into discipline and focus, the three are interwoven much like a threefold cord

Ecclesiastes 4:12 speaks of a threefold cord saying

that it is not quickly broken. One of those traits is good. Two of those traits is better. All three traits are best! Remember the acronym DDF, it is simple to say and easy to remember. Saying it often triggers focus for me.

WEEK 47

Flip It!

You've heard many expressions, slogans, and terms that include the word "flip." People flip houses, flip scripts, and flip money. It is important to understand how "flipping" applies to all aspects of a person's life. Some people use the term "re-up," which follows the same principle. You must consistently take the things you create and set aside a portion of what you receive to build something else. Always plan to build something new. Never stop planning to create more than what you currently have. Additionally, I encourage you to partner with others of like mind. Keep flipping your gifts, talents, wisdom, and resources to create bigger and better things that will impact your family and the world for the better.

In Mark 10:29 Jesus replying to Peter who spoke about the disciples leaving all their possessions to follow him said, "Verily I say unto you, there is no man that haft left house, or brethren, or sisters, or father, or mother, or wife, or children, or lands, for my sake, and the gospel's, but he shall receive an hundredfold now in this time, houses, and brethren, and sisters, and mothers, and children, and lands, with persecutions; and in the world to come eternal life."

Jesus is talking about those who sacrifice to follow Him and take possession of the calling God has placed on their lives. Sacrifice is often required to develop the talents and gifts that you possess. God blesses the sacrifices we make to further His causes.

WEEK 48

The Power Wrapped Inside Personal Discipline

You can change your life through personal commitment and personal discipline. Personal commitment is the confession that comes from your heart. It is the light that guides you to positive change. Discipline is the work that goes with your personal commitment confession. Because of a grateful heart, each day we rise, our first thoughts must be those personal commitment confessions. If you must, write them out and keep them close to you at all times. These statements should guide your work and your actions toward yourself and others. If you wake up every day and do the work that is a direct reflection of your personal commitment confessions, you will experience living your purpose. Doing this epitomizes the phrase that Ice Cube made famous: "Check yourself."

The practice of discipline in your life is one of the ways you can be sure that God loves you. Hebrews 12:6 (AMP) says, "For the Lord corrects and disciplines everyone that He loves, and He punishes, even scourges, every son whom He accepts and welcomes to His heart and cherishes." If discipline is a sure sign of God's love, should it not also be part of loving ourselves. Self- discipline is a sure sign of mature self-love.

WEEK 49

Become the Best Listener in the Room No Matter What Room You Are In

Greatness and the information that leads to it are around you. It's everywhere. It is inside many of the people already in your life. It is not an exclusive club. It does not discriminate. In fact, true wisdom often comes from the depth and diversity of the sources you receive information from. When you listen to different points of view about a dilemma or problem, you will be able to take proper actions that will produce the correct solution. Therefore, it is critical to become the best listener in the room. Learn to listen in a way that allows you to follow up with critical questions that move you closer to a successful outcome.

In Job, Chapter 32, there was a young man who waited for the elders to finish speaking. The passage about Elihu (the young man) goes on to say, "I said, days should speak, and multitude of years should teach wisdom. But there is a spirit in man and the inspiration of the Almighty giveth them understanding. Great men are not always wise: neither do the aged understand judgment." Wisdom can come from anyone who is tuned to God's channel. Wisdom is one of those things that God is prepared to give us liberally, if we ask as it states in James 1:5.

WEEK 50

Quitting Isn't the Answer

Sometimes, we are tired and exhausted. We want to give up or give in to the forces that try to defeat us. In times of great trial and challenge, we must find our inner strength. We must connect to the inner circle of the people we trust. Even in times of despair, we must go forward. Beyond our darkest times are life's greatest rewards. During dark and difficult situations, seek to revive, survive, and then you can thrive again.

Thought:

Continuous courage is the rugged all-terrain vehicle by which the mountain of fear is climbed and conquered.

Perseverance is often the word used when we talk about having the power to withstand the challenges that take most people down. Sometimes, it seems that we can fight no more and that all we can do is stand. Then, stand we must!

In Exodus 14, the children of Israel were

complaining that Moses had only brought them out of Egypt to die in the wilderness. The Egyptians were closing in on them and they feared they would be killed. Moses said to the children of Israel, "Fear ye not, standstill, and see the salvation of the Lord, which he will shew to you today." These were Moses' words right before he lifted his rod and God parted the Red Sea. Even when going on seems impossible, keep going. Even when there is no more fight in you, stand still! God may just part your own Red Sea.

WEEK 51

Think Big! Or Stay Small

It is rare to start something that is immediately large and successful. Usually, what we begin starts small and grows. Yet, I encourage you to think big. Thinking big helps keep you inspired. Thinking big helps fuel your hopes and often your creativity. Thinking big means finding the balance between big creative thinking and the practicality of being a good steward of what God has already blessed you with. The fuel of inspired creative thinking can create a way where there seemed to be no way!

Upon God's orders, Noah built a large ship. He was between 500 and 600 years old. The ship was large enough to carry Noah's family and male and female creatures of every kind. It was not an overnight process; it took decades of work. Noah was 600 years old when the floods came to destroy everything. Because Noah carried out this huge task, he saved his family and condemned evil in the manner God directed him to. Think BIG, but have the required patience it takes to see the manifestation of the promises of God.

WEEK 52

Does What Anyone Else Thinks Really Matter?

Are you seeking validation from someone? Are you seeking permission from someone? Are you mimicking someone at the expense of not becoming what you are called to be? True validation only comes from the One who gave you the assignment. If other people have no part in financing or supporting your venture, you don't need their permission. Do not measure yourself by the standards or successes of others. The gift of a life assignment is unique to you alone. It is given to you with your purpose and destiny in mind.

Family members, spouses, and close friends are often put in your life to build you up and help you see your assignment. Yet, there can also be family and friends who are close to you but do not clearly see you or your assignment. Identify those who do see you — the real you. These individuals can be a source of encouragement and great advice. Those who can't see who you really are have no bearing on what you are called to do. At worst, they may say or do things that cause you to question your faith and weaken your confidence almost every time you see them. At best, they are a neutral force in your life.

Why make room in your life for people who don't move you forward? The people around you should make you a better version of yourself, and you should do the same for them.

In Galatians 1:10 (NIV) Paul states, "Am I now trying to win the approval of human beings, or of God? Or am I trying to please people? If I were still trying to please people, I would not be a servant of God."

We must focus our attention on pleasing and taking guidance from the One that counts. The other people and things in our lives are taken care of by first seeking God.

A COLLECTION OF WORDS

TO PONDER ALONG YOUR JOURNEY

Believe

Plan

Vision

Drive

Passion

Wisdom

Failure

Perseverance

Patience

Victory

Change

Design

Love

Empower

Fight

Trust

What will these words mean as they come up along your journey? Undoubtedly, they will mean different things to different people under a variety of circumstances. These words will be a part of the successful narrative that is your life. The spirit embodied in these words will impact each and every life on this earth and, with certainty, some or all will impact yours.

Love – Life – Faith – Power – Conviction

To Your Calling

A very special thank you to my friend, John Demshock, for the beautiful nature photography. The purpose of these images is not to align with the subject matter but to open the mind to the beauty and brilliance of creation, fostering a more receptive mindset for the ideas in this book. Thank you, JD!

www.ingramcontent.com/pod-product-compliance
Lightning Source LLC
Chambersburg PA
CBHW051218120626
46547CB00013B/1413